D0191582

The Power of a
PRAYING®
Grandparent
BOOK OF PRAYERS

STORMIE OMARTIAN

HARVEST HOUSE PUBLISHERS
EUGENE, OREGON

Cover design by Nicole Dougherty

Back cover author photo © Michael Gomez Photography

Cover Image © Komar art / Shutterstock

THE POWER OF A PRAYING is a registered trademark of The Hawkins Children's LLC. Harvest House Publishers, Inc., is the exclusive licensee of the federally registered trademark THE POWER OF A PRAYING.

THE POWER OF A PRAYING® GRANDPARENT BOOK OF PRAYERS
Copyright © 2016 by Stormie Omartian
Published by Harvest House Publishers
Eugene, Oregon 97402
www.harvesthousepublishers.com

ISBN 978-0-7369-6304-6 (pbk.)
ISBN 978-0-7369-6305-3 (eBook)
ISBN 978-0-7369-7105-8 (Milano Softone™)

Printed in China

22 23 / RDS-CD / 10 9 8 7 6 5 4 3 2

Introduction

From the moment we hear that we are going to be a grandparent, something happens in our heart that makes room for this special person. And when we see him or her for the first time, the love we have in us grows dramatically beyond what we thought it could. It is unconditional, unfailing, and unshakable. With it comes a sense that we must cover this precious child in prayer.

Having lived as long as we have, we grandparents have learned a thing or two and are able to clearly see the challenges, dangers, and roadblocks to safety and happiness. Our first thoughts are to pray for our grandchild's protection. And that we must do. But there is much more to pray about as well. How do we remember it all?

I have made it easy for you in this little prayer book by giving you prayers that include the most important aspects of your grandchild's life. As you pray each prayer, add on specific prayer needs for your grandchild as the Lord brings them to mind. Included in these prayers for your grandchildren are also a few for you as a grandmother or grandfather, and a few for the parents of each of your grandchildren. In fact, one of the best gifts you can give your grandchildren is to pray for their parents.

The Bible says that good grandparents leave an inheritance to their grandchildren. Your prayers can leave a spiritual inheritance of blessings that are far greater than any material possession.

Stormie Omartian

A good man leaves an inheritance to his children's children.

PROVERBS 13:22

Lord, Enable Me to Clearly Express Love for Each of My Grandchildren

Lord, I lift up my grandchildren to You. (<u>Name each grandchild before God.</u>) Show me how to express my deep, unconditional love for each of them in a way they can clearly perceive and receive. Reveal to me the many ways I can demonstrate my love for each child. If there is a place in my heart where I feel rejected or unloved, I bring that to You for healing. I don't want to carry anything in my heart that shouldn't be there. Set me completely free from all unforgiveness today so there is no mountain of separation between me and my children or grandchildren. Keep my heart clean so that my prayers are never hindered.

In Jesus' name I pray.

If we love one another, God abides in us,
and His love has been perfected in us.

1 John 4:12

Prayer Notes

Lord, Enable Me to Clearly Express Love for Each of My Grandchildren

Lord, if there are any strongholds of separation or breaches of relationships in my family, dissolve those completely. Burn away any barriers to total forgiveness in the hearts of the people involved. Help me to pray so powerfully for my grandchildren that they sense Your love and mine for them. Enable my prayers to touch them deeply and create a bond of love between us. Enable me to be one of the "peacemakers" You have described in Your Word. I know that functioning in that role distinguishes me as a child of Yours (Matthew 5:9). I pray for Your peace that passes all understanding to reign in my family—and the families of my children and grandchildren.

In Jesus' name I pray.

Walk worthy of the calling with which you were called, with all lowliness and gentleness, with longsuffering, bearing with one another in love, endeavoring to keep the unity of the Spirit in the bond of peace.

EPHESIANS 4:1-3

Prayer Notes

Lord, Grow Love in My Grandchildren's Parents for Their Children and Each Other

Lord, I lift up to You my grandchildren's parents. (Name each parent before God.) Help them to get along as a couple and not allow strife or arguments to pull them apart. Teach them to seek harmony, unity, and peace in their home every day. I pray they will love each other and not allow a spirit of divorce to break up their family. I know You hear my prayers, and You can enable someone I pray for to better hear from You—if he or she desires to do so. I pray that each parent of my grandchildren will be able to express love for his or her children in ways that can be clearly perceived so that the children always feel loved.

In Jesus' name I pray.

Beloved, let us love one another, for love is of God; and everyone who loves is born of God and knows God.

1 John 4:7

Prayer Notes

_____

_____

_____

_____

_____

_____

_____

_____

_____

_____

_____

_____

Lord, Grow Love in My Grandchildren's Parents for Their Children and Each Other

Lord, fill my grandchildren's parents with Your love so that it overflows from them to their children. Give them obvious signs of love—such as mercy, forgiveness, patience, generosity of heart, acceptance, and encouragement—not only for their children, but also for one another. Remind them to make their children a priority, next to their love for You and each other. Give them the ability to communicate their love to their children in a way that makes it clear to them. I pray that the parents will never use their children to punish each other or the grandparents because of a spirit of revenge, which is totally against Your will. Help them to put their children's needs first before themselves.

In Jesus' name I pray.

*The fruit of the Spirit is love, joy, peace,
longsuffering, kindness, goodness,
faithfulness, gentleness, self-control.
Against such there is no law.*

GALATIANS 5:22-23

Prayer Notes

Lord, Help My Grandchildren Understand How Much You Love Them

Lord, pour out Your love on my grandchildren. (<u>Name each grandchild before God.</u>) I pray that my grandchildren will know You well and have hearts that are filled with Your love, peace, and joy so they will live peaceful lives. Help them "to know the love of Christ which passes knowledge" so that they will experience the fullness of all that You are, and all that You have for them (Ephesians 3:19). Open their hearts to trust that nothing can separate them from Your love. That's because when they say they are sorry to You and promise to not do it again, You forgive them. Help my grandchildren learn that when we look to You first, You provide everything we need because You love us.

In Jesus' name I pray.

*I am persuaded that neither death nor life,
nor angels nor principalities nor powers, nor
things present nor things to come, nor height
nor depth, nor any other created thing, shall
be able to separate us from the love of God
which is in Christ Jesus our Lord.*

ROMANS 8:38-39

Prayer Notes

Lord, Help My Grandchildren Understand How Much You Love Them

Lord, help me teach my grandchildren in a way they can understand that Your Word says to "seek first the kingdom of God and His righteousness," and all we need will be given to us (Matthew 6:33). And to "taste and see that the LORD is good; blessed is the man who trusts in Him!" (Psalm 34:8). Also that "there is no want to those who fear Him" (verse 9). And "those who seek the LORD shall not lack any good thing" (verse 10). Help me to explain to them that when they draw close to You, You draw close to them and they are never alone. Help them understand that You care so much about every detail of their lives that You want them to talk to You in prayer every day.

In Jesus' name I pray.

Our soul waits for the LORD; He is our help and our shield. For our heart shall rejoice in Him, because we have trusted in His holy name. Let Your mercy, O LORD, be upon us, just as we hope in You.

PSALM 33:20-22

Prayer Notes

Lord, Instruct My Grandchildren to Honor Their Father and Mother

Lord, I lift up my grandchildren to You. (Name each grandchild before God.) I pray that You would teach them how to honor their parents. Help their parents to understand why it is important to require that of their children and not allow them to rule the family. Give the parents understanding as to how important this is to their children's quality and length of life. I know that every child will test the boundaries, so I pray that the parents will make the boundaries clear. Give each parent the ability to be consistent with his or her rules and requirements without being hardhearted and loveless. Give them love and the ability to care responsibly for their children so that their children don't become frustrated and angry.

In Jesus' name I pray.

Children, obey your parents in all things,
for this is well pleasing to the Lord.

Colossians 3:20

Prayer Notes

Lord, Instruct My Grandchildren to Honor Their Father and Mother

Lord, give each of my grandchildren the desire to live a long and good life that comes by honoring his or her father and mother, which also honors You. Help me to encourage them to do that, and show me ways I can reinforce that attitude of respect. When my grandchildren stay with me, help me to honor their parents' instructions and requests so that I never encourage them to be disobedient in any way to their parents' rules and requirements. Give me words that build up who their parents are and how much they deserve respect. If any one of my grandchildren is grown up and forgiveness is needed between him and his parents, I pray You would open the door for that.

In Jesus' name I pray.

*Honor your father and your mother, that
your days may be long upon the land which
the LORD your God is giving you.*

Exodus 20:12

Prayer Notes

Lord, Give Each of My Grandchildren a Heart That Is Quick to Forgive

Lord, I lift up my grandchildren to You. (<u>Name each grandchild before God.</u>) I pray that each of them will have a heart that is quick to forgive. Let no root of bitterness creep into the heart of any grandchild because he or she refused to let an offense go. Help my grandchildren to understand how far-reaching Your love, mercy, and forgiveness are, and how much You want them to be loving, merciful, and forgiving to others. Reveal any place in their heart and mind where they have not forgiven someone or have placed blame for something bad that happened and not let go of it. Don't let them carry anything in their heart that will hinder their ability to receive all of the blessings You have for them.

In Jesus' name I pray.

I say to you, love your enemies, bless those
who curse you, do good to those who hate
you, and pray for those who spitefully use
you and persecute you, that you may be sons
of your Father in heaven.

MATTHEW 5:44-45

Prayer Notes

Lord, Give Each of My Grandchildren a Heart That Is Quick to Forgive

Lord, help my grandchildren's parents to be forgiving people. Where there is any lack of forgiveness in their hearts—especially toward each other—I pray You would bring that stronghold of torture down to nothing. Cause them to refuse to perpetuate it any longer. Open their hearts to recognize the damage unforgiveness causes and help them to determine not to live that way any longer. Make me to be a good and godly influence on my grandchildren. Show me how to guide them in the way of love, mercy, and forgiveness. Teach them to learn to forgive quickly and completely so they are never tortured by unforgiveness—and Your plan for their lives is never hindered.

In Jesus' name I pray.

Be kind to one another, tenderhearted,
forgiving one another, just as God in Christ
forgave you.

EPHESIANS 4:32

Prayer Notes

Lord, Teach My Grandchildren Ways to Show Their Love for You

Lord, I lift up my grandchildren to You. (<u>Name each grandchild before God.</u>) Help them to understand how good You are—all the time. Help them to learn how You forgive us, heal us, save us from destruction, show us kindness, and are always loving and merciful toward us. Help each grandchild to understand who You really are so that they will learn to love You above all else. I pray that the clear knowledge of who You are will cause them to never allow anyone or anything to come between them and their love for You. Help them to think of You as their greatest treasure so that they will make room in their heart for You, and in their life for all You have for them.

In Jesus' name I pray.

It is good to give thanks to the LORD, and to sing praises to Your name, O Most High; to declare Your lovingkindness in the morning, and Your faithfulness every night.

PSALM 92:1-2

Prayer Notes

_____

_____

_____

_____

_____

_____

_____

_____

_____

_____

_____

Lord, Teach My Grandchildren Ways to Show Their Love for You

Lord, Your Word says, "One generation shall praise Your works to another, and shall declare Your mighty acts" (Psalm 145:4). Teach my grandchildren all the ways they can show their love for You. Thank You that as they praise You, it opens up their heart for You to pour more of Your love, joy, and peace into them. Your Word says, "Where your treasure is, there your heart will be also" (Matthew 6:21). Help my grandchildren to make You their greatest treasure. Enable me to teach them that we love You because You "first loved us," and loving You is the first and most important thing we do in our lives (1 John 4:19).

In Jesus' name I pray.

I will praise You with my whole heart...for
Your lovingkindness and Your truth.

Psalm 138:1-2

Prayer Notes

Lord, Reveal to My Grandchildren How to Love Others the Way You Do

Lord, I lift up my grandchildren to You. (Name each grandchild before God.) I ask that You would put love in each child's heart for other people, especially for his or her family members and friends, but also for people who are not easy to love. Help my grandchildren to learn to love others the way You do. Help us all as a family to forsake envy, pride, rudeness, selfishness, and criticism—which reveal a lack of love for others—so we can learn to "walk in love, as Christ also has loved us" (Ephesians 5:2). Teach my grandchildren to understand Your commandment to love others. Let their love for others be the most important sign that they know You, love You, and serve You.

In Jesus' name I pray.

This commandment we have from Him:
that he who loves God must love
his brother also.

1 JOHN 4:21

Prayer Notes

_____

_____

_____

_____

_____

_____

_____

_____

_____

_____

_____

_____

Lord, Reveal to My Grandchildren How to Love Others the Way You Do

Lord, enable my grandchildren to understand that love is what gives meaning to everything they do. Help them know that one of the greatest gifts of love they can give anyone is to pray for them. If there is ever a friend, family member, acquaintance, or neighbor who is troubling or hateful to them, teach them to pray for that person and release them into Your hands. Instead of thinking of retribution, show them that praying for those difficult people to have a life-changing encounter with You is actually the best revenge. Grow each of my grandchildren to be a person whose heart is filled to overflowing with Your love for other people. Help me to always model that as well.

In Jesus' name I pray.

*Let no one seek his own, but each one the
other's well-being.*

1 Corinthians 10:24

Prayer Notes

_____

_____

_____

_____

_____

_____

_____

_____

_____

_____

_____

_____

Lord, Teach Me to See the Inheritance I Leave as a Praying Grandparent

Lord, I lift up my grandchildren to You. (<u>Name each grandchild before God.</u>) Help me to clearly see the spiritual inheritance I leave each one when I pray for them. Thank You for all of the wonderful promises in Your Word that declare You will bless my children and grandchildren when I live Your way. I know that children are a gift from You and grandchildren are a crown of glory upon my life (Proverbs 17:6). I know that whether I can see my grandchildren often or not, I can still be close to them every time I pray for them. Thank You that You hear "the prayer of the righteous" (Proverbs 15:29). I am righteous because I have received You, Jesus, and I love and serve You.

In Your name I pray.

*The silver-haired head is a crown of glory,
if it is found in the way of righteousness.*

PROVERBS 16:31

Prayer Notes

_____

_____

_____

_____

_____

_____

_____

_____

_____

_____

_____

Lord, Teach Me to See the Inheritance I Leave as a Praying Grandparent

Lord, Your Word says my children and their children "will be established before You" (Psalm 102:28). I know that "a good man leaves an inheritance to his children's children" (Proverbs 13:22). Thank You that there is an inheritance I can leave my children and grandchildren that is even more valuable than possessions, and that precious gift is a spiritual inheritance that will help them to be established on a good foundation. Help me to live in obedience to Your commandments so that I can leave a great spiritual inheritance to my children and grandchildren. Thank You that my prayers for them are lasting, so that when I have left this earth to be with You, the effects of my prayers will still be felt.

In Jesus' name I pray.

In Him also we have obtained an inheritance,
being predestined according to the purpose
of Him who works all things according
to the counsel of His will.

EPHESIANS 1:11

Prayer Notes

Lord, Help My Grandchildren's Parents to Raise Them Your Way

Lord, I lift my grandchildren's parents, step-parents, or guardians up to You. (Name each one before God.) I pray that they will know how to teach each child to obey not only them, but also all who are in authority in their lives, such as teachers and law enforcement people. Instruct the parents to live Your way so that they can teach their children to live Your way as well. I pray that if a parent does not know You, You will open his or her mind to see Your truth and open his or her heart to receive Your life. Teach my grandchildren's parents Your laws and enable them to teach Your ways to their children as well.

In Jesus' name I pray.

Fathers, do not provoke your children to
wrath, but bring them up in the training
and admonition of the Lord.

Ephesians 6:4

Prayer Notes

Lord, Help My Grandchildren's Parents to Raise Them Your Way

Lord, enable my grandchildren's parents to realize that they cannot raise their children well without You. Enable them to know how to discipline their children promptly in love and in proper ways. Help them not to be too lenient so that their children become spoiled and unruly. And keep them from being too strict so that their children's hearts and spirits are not broken.

Give the parents godly wisdom so they can make good decisions regarding each child. I pray they will invite You to be in charge of their children and seek Your help to bring them up in Your ways. Instruct them to teach their children Your Word so that they will live a long and good life.

In Jesus' name I pray.

I have taught you in the way of wisdom;
I have led you in right paths. When you walk,
your steps will not be hindered, and when
you run, you will not stumble.

PROVERBS 4:11-12

Prayer Notes

_____

_____

_____

_____

_____

_____

_____

_____

_____

_____

Lord, Protect My Grandchildren from Any Danger or Threat

Lord, I pray for my grandchildren. (<u>Name each grandchild before God</u>.) I ask that You would put Your hand of protection upon them. Keep them safe from accidents or dangers of any kind. Surround them with Your angels. I know that "You alone" can make them to "dwell in safety" (Psalm 4:8). Help them to understand that You are their protector, and You can keep them safe when they live Your way and seek Your hand of protection. Enable them to see that when they go their own way, without regard for Your way, they walk out from under Your umbrella of protection. Give them no peace about going anyplace, or doing anything, that will expose them or others to danger.

In Jesus' name I pray.

Because you have made the LORD, who is my refuge, even the Most High, your dwelling place, no evil shall befall you, nor shall any plague come near your dwelling.

PSALM 91:9-10

Prayer Notes

Lord, Protect My Grandchildren from Any Danger or Threat

Lord, I pray that my grandchildren will always live in safe neighborhoods with godly neighbors. Teach my grandchildren to be a blessing to their neighbors and to people in their school, workplace, and wherever they go. Give all who care for them the ability to see ahead what the dangers are. Protect my grandchildren in cars, planes, trains, buses, on bicycles, and in any other form of transportation. Watch over them wherever they walk and in whatever activity they are involved in. Whenever I'm around them, make me aware of all possible dangers as well. Thank You, Lord, that I can have peace because I know that You protect us and help us to live securely when we pray and live Your way.

In Jesus' name I pray.

He shall give His angels charge over you,
to keep you in all your ways.

Psalm 91:11

Prayer Notes

_____

_____

_____

_____

_____

_____

_____

_____

_____

_____

_____

_____

_____

Lord, Heal My Grandchildren from Every Disease and Infirmity

Lord, I pray for my grandchildren to have good health all the days of their lives. Protect them from wasting and devastating diseases. Specifically, I pray for (name each grandchild and anything that concerns you about his or her physical health). You've said in Your Word that "My people are destroyed for lack of knowledge" (Hosea 4:6). Don't let my grandchildren be destroyed because they or their parents lack knowledge about how to take care of their bodies. Give them the desire to eat healthful food. I know that any child left to himself will most likely eat enticing food that can do more harm than good. Give my grandchildren the gift of good sense and a desire for food that will bless their bodies with health.

In Jesus' name I pray.

*Whether you eat or drink, or whatever you
do, do all to the glory of God.*

1 Corinthians 10:31

Prayer Notes

_____

_____

_____

_____

_____

_____

_____

_____

_____

_____

_____

_____

Lord, Heal My Grandchildren from Every Disease and Infirmity

Lord, help my grandchildren to consider the condition of their health seriously and not take good health for granted. Teach them that they cannot think they will forever get away with doing whatever they want. Help them to turn to You for guidance as to what they should do and should not do in order to maintain good health. I pray they will learn to take care of their bodies with proper exercise and rest. Help them make choices to not allow bad things into their bodies that will harm them, such as drugs, alcohol, cigarettes, and junk food. Take away all attraction for anything that will make them sick. Help them to love their body and be thankful to You for all it can do.

In Jesus' name I pray.

He was wounded for our transgressions,
He was bruised for our iniquities;
the chastisement for our peace was upon
Him, and by His stripes we are healed.

ISAIAH 53:5

Prayer Notes

_____

_____

_____

_____

_____

_____

_____

_____

_____

_____

_____

Lord, Give My Grandchildren Good and Wise Doctors

Lord, I lift up my grandchildren to You. (<u>Name each grandchild before God.</u>) I ask that You will provide each of them with good, excellent, and wise doctors, nurses, medical technicians, and physical therapists to treat them as needed. Keep my grandchildren from ever being misdiagnosed or given improper treatment. Give discernment to every doctor they see so that my grandchildren are never prescribed the wrong drug and given medicine that will do damage to them in any way. If there is ever a misdiagnosis, reveal it right away so that proper treatment can be given. Give all of their doctors the wisdom and good judgment needed to do what is best for my grandchildren.

In Jesus' name I pray.

Heal me, O LORD, and I shall be healed;
save me, and I shall be saved,
for You are my praise.

JEREMIAH 17:14

Prayer Notes

Lord, Give My Grandchildren Good and Wise Doctors

Lord, if there is ever a shroud of mystery over any health problem my grandchildren may have, I pray You would remove it. Make known the truth for all to see—especially to doctors and other medical personnel. You always know exactly what the problem is and can not only reveal it, but also clarify what needs to be done about it. Give my grandchildren's parents the means to pay for all necessary medical treatments. Provide insurance and medical aid for them so they can always get help. Give me the means to assist in any way I can as well. Give my grandchildren and their parents a sense of peace when they are seeing the right doctor and the diagnosis is correct. Give them wisdom for every decision they must make.

In Jesus' name I pray.

"I will restore health to you and heal you of your wounds," says the Lord.

JEREMIAH 30:17

Prayer Notes

Lord, Give My Grandchildren Good and Wise Doctors

Lord, I also pray for godly wisdom for my grandchildren and their parents or caretakers so they will know what to do in every situation that requires medical treatment. Don't let them wait too long to get the medical care they need, and help them choose the right doctor. I pray they will not accept a bad verdict that sentences their children to a hopeless outcome. Help them to ask, seek, and knock until they have found the proper care. Keep us all from accepting the judgment of man as being higher than Your ability to heal. At the same time, don't let us live in denial about something if it is Your will that we walk through it with You.

In Jesus' name I pray.

Ask, and it will be given to you; seek, and you will find; knock, and it will be opened to you. For everyone who asks receives, and he who seeks finds, and to him who knocks it will be opened.

MATTHEW 7:7-8

Prayer Notes

Lord, Keep My Grandchildren Far from the Harm of Evil People

Lord, I lift up my grandchildren to You. (<u>Name each grandchild before God.</u>) I ask that You would protect each of them from all evil people—whether at school, or daycare, or wherever they are—with babysitters, neighbors, camp counselors, family members, coworkers, or friends who have bad intentions toward them. I pray that my grandchildren will never be abused in any way. Deliver them from evil, and reveal any potential abuser before anything bad happens. Where evil people lurk, expose their plans. Give my grandchildren the discernment and wisdom to know when people are not trustworthy. Enable them to sense evil quickly if it comes near them. Help them to immediately identify when someone is doing anything inappropriate.

In Jesus' name I pray.

You, O LORD, will bless the righteous; with favor You will surround him as with a shield.

PSALM 5:12

Prayer Notes

Lord, Keep My Grandchildren Far from the Harm of Evil People

Lord, keep my grandchildren from being intimidated by the threats of those people who want to do them harm. If any abuse or contact with evil people has already happened, I pray You would bring the perpetrators to light. Expose their evil actions in a court of law, and let them be punished for their crimes. Lead the parents of that grandchild to find professional help for their child so that they can fully recover what has been lost and heal whatever has been broken in them as a result. Surround my grandchildren with Your angels so that no person intending to do evil to them will ever find an opportunity to do so.

In Jesus' name I pray.

Surely He shall deliver you from the snare of the fowler and from the perilous pestilence. He shall cover you with His feathers, and under His wings you shall take refuge; His truth shall be your shield and buckler.

PSALM 91:3-4

Prayer Notes

Lord, Let No Weapon Prosper That Is Formed Against My Grandchildren

Lord, I lift my grandchildren up to You. (<u>Name each grandchild before God.</u>) I see that evil is all around us, and so I pray You will always protect my children and grandchildren from it. Send Your angels to guard them and protect them from any plans of the evil one. Break down any strongholds the enemy tries to erect against them. Thank You for Your Word that says to Your people who love and serve You that "no weapon formed against you shall prosper" (Isaiah 54:17). Where something bad has already happened to one of my grandchildren, I pray You will bring restoration to that child and to the entire family so that the enemy will be entirely defeated.

In Jesus' name I pray.

*When the whirlwind passes by, the wicked is
no more, but the righteous has
an everlasting foundation.*

PROVERBS 10:25

Prayer Notes

_____

_____

_____

_____

_____

_____

_____

_____

_____

_____

_____

Lord, Let No Weapon Prosper That Is Formed Against My Grandchildren

Lord, thank You that Your Word says that we who believe in You have "an everlasting foundation" (Proverbs 10:25). I claim the foundation I have in You, and I stand on Your side in this war between good and evil. Your enemy is also mine, and I choose to do battle against him in prayer as You have required. Thank You that "You have armed me with strength for the battle" (Psalm 18:39). Help me to take up the sword of the Spirit—Your Word—every day because it is my greatest weapon against the enemy. Enable me to be led by Your Holy Spirit as I pray. Enable me to be an unshakable prayer warrior for my children and grandchildren in whatever way You lead me.

In Jesus' name I pray.

*The word of God is living and powerful, and
sharper than any two-edged sword, piercing
even to the division of soul and spirit, and of
joints and marrow, and is a discerner of the
thoughts and intents of the heart.*

HEBREWS 4:12

Prayer Notes

Lord, Enable Me to Understand What My Grandchildren Face in This World

Lord, I am very concerned for the future of my grandchildren. (<u>Name each grandchild before God.</u>) I cannot bear the thought of any of the things I see happening in this world happening to them. I can only have peace knowing that You will keep them safe from what is ahead. I pray they will stay close to You and hear Your voice guiding them to walk ever closer to You. Give them great pastors and youth leaders who hear from You, never disobey Your laws and commandments, and never violate their trust. I pray that each of my grandchildren will marry a godly spouse and stay happily married and raise godly children. Show me how to pray for them regarding all they will face in their lives.

In Jesus' name I pray.

The Spirit also helps in our weaknesses. For we do not know what we should pray for as we ought, but the Spirit Himself makes intercession for us with groanings which cannot be uttered.

ROMANS 8:26

Prayer Notes

_____

_____

_____

_____

_____

_____

_____

_____

_____

_____

_____

Lord, Enable Me to Understand What My Grandchildren Face in This World

Lord, I see evil and danger increasing in this world every day with no indication that it will be getting better. I know Your Word says that wickedness will increase, and people will more and more be lovers of themselves and not lovers of You and Your Word. I pray that my grandchildren will be lovers of You and Your Word and not lovers of themselves. Pierce their conscience if they consider choosing another path than the one You have for them. Your Word says that in the world we will face problems, but You "have overcome the world" (John 16:33). Thank You that You have done so much for us. Thank You that You are greater than anything I or my grandchildren or their parents will face.

In Jesus' name I pray.

These things I have spoken to you, that in Me
you may have peace. In the world you will
have tribulation; but be of good cheer,
I have overcome the world.

JOHN 16:33

Prayer Notes

_____

_____

_____

_____

_____

_____

_____

_____

_____

_____

_____

_____

Lord, Enable Me to Understand What My Grandchildren Face in This World

Lord, give me knowledge about how to pray regarding the specifics of what my grandchildren are facing now or will face in the future. Show me what it will be like in their schools, in their workplaces, in their families, and with their peers. Guide me so I can pray in advance of the things that will happen in the world around them. Only You can keep them safe and help them to accomplish great things for Your kingdom. Just as David knew to pray morning, noon, and night, help me to keep praying like that as well. Keep me from neglecting my grandchildren by ceasing to pray for them. Give me strength, health, and a clear mind until I go to be with You.

In Jesus' name I pray.

Evening and morning and at noon I will pray,
and cry aloud, and He shall hear my voice.

PSALM 55:17

Prayer Notes

Lord, Lead My Grandchildren's Parents into a Close Relationship with You

Lord, I pray that each of my grandchildren's parents will be drawn into a deep and committed relationship with You. (<u>Specifically name the parents, stepparents, or guardians of each of your grandchildren.</u>) I see in Your Word that children and grandchildren have a great advantage if their parents instruct them how to live Your way and then show them by serving You. Help these parents to fully understand Your ways and Your love and communicate them to their children. Bring godly people into the parents' lives to guide them in Your way. Lead them to a good, vibrant, Bible-believing church so that they and their children will be fed by Your Spirit and not the spirit of the world.

In Jesus' name I pray.

I have no greater joy than to hear that my children walk in truth.

3 John 4

Prayer Notes

_____

_____

_____

_____

_____

_____

_____

_____

_____

_____

_____

Lord, Lead My Grandchildren's Parents into a Close Relationship with You

Lord, give my grandchildren's parents a love for Your Word. Bring it alive to them so that the words leap off the page and into their heart to stay. Open doors to Bible studies and prayer groups so godly friendships can grow out of them. No matter where the parents are in their walk with You, bring them closer. If any of them does not know You, draw that person to receive You as his or her Savior. If they do profess to know You, bring them into a greater knowledge of who You are and what Your Word says. Give the parents wisdom in raising their children so that they impart to them a desire to live Your way.

In Jesus' name I pray.

*All your children shall be taught by the LORD,
and great shall be the peace of your children.*

ISAIAH 54:13

Prayer Notes

_____

_____

_____

_____

_____

_____

_____

_____

_____

_____

_____

_____

Lord, Draw My Grandchildren to Know You Better Every Day

Lord, draw my grandchildren close to You. (<u>Name each grandchild before God.</u>) Help them to come to know You in a deep and committed way so that their relationship with You grows every day. Teach them to understand Your laws and commandments, and help them keep Your ways faithfully. Show my grandchildren's parents and me how to communicate Your Word to them in ways they understand so that they are always drawn to it. I pray You will put Your laws in the mind and heart of each of my precious grandchildren so that they will make decisions to live Your way. Give each one a heart that wants to be closer to You so that they always sense Your presence.

In Jesus' name I pray.

The LORD is near to all who call upon Him,
to all who call upon Him in truth.

PSALM 145:18

Prayer Notes

Lord, Draw My Grandchildren to Know You Better Every Day

Lord, show me everything I can do to teach my grandchildren about who You are and all You've done. Reveal to me the examples in my own life, or the life of someone I have known, that make a powerful point about the dangers of not knowing You and not living Your way. Most of all, Lord, help me to communicate Your love to them in ways they can fully comprehend. Teach my grandchildren to be praying people. Help me to pray with them every opportunity I have. Teach their parents to pray with them too so that they grow to know the fulfillment of communicating with You. Give them a desire to grow nearer to You every day and follow You all the days of their lives. Teach them about the power of Your name.

In Jesus' name I pray.

The name of the LORD is a strong tower;
the righteous run to it and are safe.

PROVERBS 18:10

Prayer Notes

_____

_____

_____

_____

_____

_____

_____

_____

_____

_____

_____

_____

Lord, Teach My Grandchildren to Resist Rebellion in Themselves

Lord, I lift up my grandchildren to You. (<u>Name each grandchild before God.</u>) Cause each one to have a humble heart and a teachable spirit. Help them learn to be humbly submitted to You as well as to their parents and legitimate authority figures in their lives. If a rebellious attitude appears, enable their parents to recognize it immediately and have the wisdom to do what it takes to put a stop to it. Give them sharp discernment so they do not allow it to grow in their children and become established. Enable me to recognize it in my grandchildren as well and resist it mightily in prayer and in communication with that child. Take away any rebellious spirit, and give each grandchild a humble heart of reverence for You.

In Jesus' name I pray.

Hear, my son, and be wise;
and guide your heart in the way.

PROVERBS 23:19

Prayer Notes

Lord, Teach My Grandchildren to Resist Rebellion in Themselves

Lord, if any of my grandchildren have a strong will, teach them to submit their will to You and not to their own desires. Help that strong-willed child to instead become a strong leader in Your kingdom who is dependent on You. Cause them to be a force for good and not evil. Enlighten them to recognize any rebellion in themselves and totally resist it. Give them a pure heart, and take away all desire to dominate or control other people. Give the parents wisdom to not be controlled by their child. Give each of my grandchildren a heart that wants to serve You and others according to Your leading and Your will in his or her life.

In Jesus' name I pray.

They shall not labor in vain, nor bring forth children for trouble; for they shall be the descendants of the blessed of the LORD, and their offspring with them.

ISAIAH 65:23

Prayer Notes

_____

_____

_____

_____

_____

_____

_____

_____

_____

_____

_____

Lord, Keep My Grandchildren from Straying into Enemy Territory

Lord, I lift up my grandchildren before You. (<u>Name each grandchild before God.</u>) I know in Your Word You promised Your people that if they would serve You, You would bring their children back from the lands of the enemy and cause them to return to You. Because I love You and want to serve You all the days of my life, I believe this promise is for me too. Keep my grandchildren safe from the evil one. I pray that if any of my children and grandchildren stray into enemy territory, You would bring them back to You. May they follow You all the days of their lives and never turn from Your ways.

In Jesus' name I pray.

I will contend with him who contends with you, and I will save your children.

ISAIAH 49:25

Prayer Notes

Lord, Keep My Grandchildren from Straying into Enemy Territory

Lord, keep my grandchildren from in any way being blinded by the enemy's lies. Teach them to always see Your truth. Enable them to hear Your voice leading them, and silence the voice of the enemy. I pray they would understand the spiritual battle we all face and all You have done for those who resist the lure of the enemy. Give my grandchildren discernment so they can clearly differentiate between good and evil. Enable them to be strong enough to not "give place to the devil" (Ephesians 4:27). Whenever the enemy turns up the intensity of his attack on my grandchildren to lead them into his territory, help me to increase the fervency of my own prayers against him, knowing that I am on Your side and doing Your will.

In Jesus' name I pray.

Submit to God. Resist the devil
and he will flee from you.

JAMES 4:7

Prayer Notes

Lord, Cause My Grandchildren to Be Attracted to Godly Friends

Lord, I lift up my grandchildren to You. (<u>Name each grandchild before God.</u>) I know how the wrong friends can lead them away from You and Your ways. Please keep that from happening with my grandchildren. Your Word says a great deal about the benefits of godly friends, so Your warning is clear. Lead them to good schools and good churches where godly friends can be found. Take away from my grandchildren any attraction in them toward friends who will cause them to stray away from the path You have for them. Disturb their conscience so badly that they will refuse to seek the acceptance of people who will draw them away from You and Your ways.

In Jesus' name I pray.

*The righteous should choose his friends
carefully, for the way of the wicked
leads them astray.*

PROVERBS 12:26

Prayer Notes

_____

_____

_____

_____

_____

_____

_____

_____

_____

_____

_____

_____

Lord, Cause My Grandchildren to Be Attracted to Godly Friends

Lord, I ask that You will bring godly friends into the lives of my grandchildren. Give them a clear vision of the consequences of spending time with ungodly friends that could lead to their destruction. Cause them to refuse to go down that path. Where friends who are a bad influence have already entered their life, cause my grandchildren to pull away from them. Make their parents well aware of it. Give me revelation about it as well, and show me how to intercede for them. Break up those friendships and remove any bad influence from their life. Do not allow the plans of evil to succeed in any one of my grandchildren through the influence of ungodly friends.

In Jesus' name I pray.

He who walks with wise men will be wise,
but the companion of fools will be destroyed.

PROVERBS 13:20

Prayer Notes

Lord, Give My Grandchildren Godly Wisdom and Understanding

Lord, I pray You will pour out Your Spirit of wisdom upon my grandchildren. (<u>Name each grandchild before God.</u>) Your Word says, "If you cry out for discernment, and lift up your voice for understanding, if you seek her as silver, and search for her as for hidden treasures; then you will understand the fear of the LORD, and find the knowledge of God" (Proverbs 2:3-5). I cry out for discernment on my grandchildren's behalf. Give them a desire for godly understanding. Cause them to seek You for wisdom. I know from Your Word that wisdom comes through Your Holy Spirit. Give them wisdom to walk away from danger and evil. Help them hear Your voice telling them which way to go (Isaiah 30:21).

In Jesus' name I pray.

When wisdom enters your heart,
and knowledge is pleasant to your soul,
discretion will preserve you; understanding
will keep you, to deliver you from the way of
evil, from the man who speaks perverse things.

PROVERBS 2:10-12

Prayer Notes

Lord, Give My Grandchildren Godly Wisdom and Understanding

Lord, give my grandchildren the wisdom they need to determine the true character of the people around them so they don't allow evil people into their lives. "The fear of the LORD is the instruction of wisdom, and before honor is humility" (Proverbs 15:33). For my grandchildren I ask as Paul did that "you may be filled with the knowledge of His will in all wisdom and spiritual understanding," and that "you may walk worthy of the Lord, fully pleasing Him, being fruitful in every good work and increasing in the knowledge of God" (Colossians 1:9-10). I pray that You, Lord, will deliver my grandchildren from the powerful darkness of ignorance and carry them into Your "kingdom of the Son of [Your] love" (Colossians 1:13).

In Jesus' name I pray.

The fear of the LORD is the beginning of wisdom, and the knowledge of the Holy One is understanding.

PROVERBS 9:10

Prayer Notes

Lord, Help Me to Be a Godly Role Model for My Grandchildren

Lord, I lift up my grandchildren to You. (<u>Name each grandchild before God.</u>) Help me to be a godly and great role model for them. Etch Your Word in my heart so deeply that I not only understand it and retain it, but it will become so much a part of me that it overflows to my children and grandchildren in the way I live and talk. Show me how to impart Your Word to each of my grandchildren in lovely and edifying ways so that it becomes part of them and is engraved on their heart. Enable me to always speak it as a blessing they love to hear and not a judgment that turns their heart off to it.

In Jesus' name I pray.

*Take heed to yourself, and diligently keep
yourself, lest you forget the things your eyes
have seen, and lest they depart from your
heart all the days of your life. And teach them
to your children and your grandchildren.*

DEUTERONOMY 4:9

Prayer Notes

_____

_____

_____

_____

_____

_____

_____

_____

_____

_____

_____

_____

Lord, Help Me to Be a Godly Role Model for My Grandchildren

Lord, help me to live a long and healthy life so I can be a positive, loving, and active influence on my grandchildren. Your Word says that the "children of Your servants will continue, and their descendants will be established before You" (Psalm 102:28). I pray that promise for my family. I pray that each one of my grandchildren—even those not yet born—will serve You every day of their lives. Enable me to always "continue earnestly in prayer, being vigilant in it with thanksgiving" (Colossians 4:2). Help me to lay such a foundation for them in Your Word and in prayer that even after I have gone to be with You, the foundation of Your Word will serve them well.

In Jesus' name I pray.

Their descendants shall be known among the Gentiles, and their offspring among the people. All who see them shall acknowledge them, that they are the posterity whom the LORD has blessed.

ISAIAH 61:9

Prayer Notes

Lord, Give the Parents of My Grandchildren the Ability to Provide Well for Their Family

Lord, I lift up my grandchildren's parents to You. (<u>Name each parent before God.</u>) I pray these parents will always have good work, and that their work will be blessed with success and financial rewards. Protect them from poverty, but also keep them from the kind of wealth that could draw their hearts away from You. Help them to understand that You are their provider so that they are always thankful to You for all You have given them, but they must still work diligently to do what You have called them to do. I pray they will seek You for provision in their lives and also give back to You and to others as You lead them.

In Jesus' name I pray.

The labor of the righteous leads to life.

PROVERBS 10:16

Prayer Notes

_____

_____

_____

_____

_____

_____

_____

_____

_____

_____

_____

Lord, Give the Parents of My Grandchildren the Ability to Provide Well for Their Family

Lord, enable my grandchildren's parents to do their work well so that they find favor with You and others. Help them to be "not lagging in diligence, fervent in spirit, serving the Lord" (Romans 12:11). I pray they will love their work and do the work they love. Don't allow them to ever neglect their children by working so hard that it occupies too much of their time. May they never sacrifice their children on the altar of their careers and cause their children to suffer because of it. You have said in Your Word that it is a gift from You to be able to enjoy our work (Ecclesiastes 3:13). I pray that my grandchildren's parents will do good work they enjoy.

In Jesus' name I pray.

*Beloved, I pray that you may prosper
in all things and be in health,
just as your soul prospers.*

3 JOHN 2

Prayer Notes

Lord, Enable My Grandchildren to Understand Who You Made Them to Be

Lord, I lift up my grandchildren to You. (<u>Name each grandchild before God.</u>) Enable each one to understand who You made them to be. Reveal to them the knowledge of who You are so they can understand who they are in relation to You. Help each grandchild to know that You are their heavenly Father and they are Your child. And as such, they have an inheritance from You. Give them a clear vision for their life and a sense of why they are here. Teach them to clearly understand that they were created for a purpose. Help them understand what that purpose is. Take away all confusion about who they are and cause them to hear Your voice to their heart telling them which way to go.

In Jesus' name I pray.

May He grant you according to your heart's desire, and fulfill all your purpose.

PSALM 20:4

Prayer Notes

Lord, Enable My Grandchildren to Understand Who You Made Them to Be

Lord, give each of my grandchildren a vision that allows a glimpse of all You have for them, so that they move through life with a sense of Your purpose. Pour out Your Spirit on them as You have spoken of in Your Word. Help them to say in their heart, "I am the LORD's" (Isaiah 44:5). Give their parents and grandparents the wisdom and knowledge they need to help them understand that they were born for a high purpose. And even if they don't yet know exactly what that is, as they seek You and walk with You, I know You will reveal it. Show me how to encourage my grandchildren about this in any way I can.

In Jesus' name I pray.

Now we have received, not the spirit of the world, but the Spirit who is from God, that we might know the things that have been freely given to us by God.

1 Corinthians 2:12

Prayer Notes

Lord, Reveal to My Grandchildren Their Gifts and Calling

Lord, I lift up my grandchildren to You. (<u>Name each grandchild before God.</u>) Thank You that You have put in each one of them special gifts and talents that are to be used for Your plans and purposes. I pray that You will enable them to live their lives with a distinctive sense of Your calling so they don't become sidetracked away from Your plans for their life. Teach them how You want their gifts to be dedicated to You and used for Your glory. Reveal that to their parents as well so they know how to nurture and develop those gifts and talents. Reveal that to me too, so I know how to pray and how to encourage them.

In Jesus' name I pray.

Having then gifts differing according to the grace that is given to us, let us use them.

Romans 12:6

Prayer Notes

Lord, Reveal to My Grandchildren Their Gifts and Calling

Lord, enable my grandchildren to hear the call You have on each of their lives. Use them to make a positive difference in the lives of others. Help me to encourage them in whatever You have called them to do. I ask that You, "the Father of glory," will give to my grandchildren the "spirit of wisdom and revelation" so they can understand Your calling on their lives (Ephesians 1:17). Help them to "walk worthy of the calling" with which they are called (Ephesians 4:1). Keep them from trying to figure out what their gifts and talents are and what Your calling is on their life. Speak to them as soon as they will listen and teach them to use their gifts according to Your will.

In Jesus' name I pray.

A man's gift makes room for him, and brings
him before great men.

PROVERBS 18:16

Prayer Notes

_____

_____

_____

_____

_____

_____

_____

_____

_____

_____

_____

_____

Lord, Reveal to My Grandchildren Their Gifts and Calling

Lord, send the right teachers, tutors, and mentors to teach and encourage my grandchildren. Open the mind, eyes, and ears of each child to help him or her clearly understand, see, and hear what You want him or her to do. Whatever any of my grandchildren are struggling with when it comes to learning, I know there is nothing You cannot work out in their lives. Help them see that their struggle doesn't mean failure. Rather, it often accomplishes in them exactly what is needed for them to succeed. Teach me to always be an encouragement to my grandchildren. Enable me to help them understand that You not only have a calling on their lives, but You will equip them to accomplish it as they depend on You.

In Jesus' name I pray.

Whom He predestined, these He also called;
whom He called, these He also justified; and
whom He justified, these He also glorified.

ROMANS 8:30

Prayer Notes

Lord, Keep Each Grandchild's Heart from Turning Toward the World's Idols

Lord, I lift up my grandchildren to You. (<u>Name each grandchild before God.</u>) Show them how to live in this world without being drawn into its darkness. Help them to separate themselves from anything that is detestable to You. Give them the strength to be led by Your Spirit and not influenced by the godless spirit in the world. Help them to reject all idols and stay separate from the traps of the enemy luring them away from all You have for them. Help my grandchildren to always remember that they are Your children. Give them a desire to be a friend of Yours and have the discernment to never want to be "an enemy of God" (James 4:4).

In Jesus' name I pray.

Do not be conformed to this world, but be transformed by the renewing of your mind, that you may prove what is that good and acceptable and perfect will of God.

ROMANS 12:2

Prayer Notes

Lord, Keep Each Grandchild's Heart from Turning Toward the World's Idols

Lord, don't let my grandchildren bring detestable things into their homes. Keep them from any person or practice that will hinder their prayers from being heard and limit them from receiving everything You have in store for them. Protect them from anything that will ultimately separate them from You and Your best in their life. "Far be it from me that I should sin against" You, Lord, "in ceasing to pray for" my grandchildren (1 Samuel 12:23). I pray they will learn to reverence You with all their heart, and to always consider what great things You have done for them (1 Samuel 12:24). I pray they will always worship You and never walk away from You to serve other gods.

In Jesus' name I pray.

You are of God, little children, and have overcome them, because He who is in you is greater than he who is in the world.

1 John 4:4

Prayer Notes

_____

_____

_____

_____

_____

_____

_____

_____

_____

_____

_____

Lord, Teach My Grandchildren How to Bear Good Fruit

Lord, I lift up each of my grandchildren before You. (<u>Name each grandchild before God.</u>) Give every one of them a soft heart for You, Your Word, and Your ways. Cause them to want to know You and serve You. Keep their heart turned toward You so that no hardness of heart can settle in on them. Watch over them and keep them from turning their back on You to live in disobedience to Your ways. If that happens, give their conscience no peace until they return to You. Holy Spirit, You are the One who convicts us of sin. Convict my grandchildren of any sin in their life and lead them to do the right thing. Make them to be a follower of only You.

In Jesus' name I pray.

In the way of righteousness is life, and in its pathway there is no death.

Proverbs 12:28

Prayer Notes

_____

_____

_____

_____

_____

_____

_____

_____

_____

_____

_____

_____

Lord, Teach My Grandchildren How to Bear Good Fruit

Lord, Your Word says, "Great peace have those who love Your law, and nothing causes them to stumble" (Psalm 119:165). Give my grandchildren deep love and respect for Your law. Pave the way for their prayers to be answered. Jesus, You said, "Ask, and it will be given to you; seek, and you will find; knock, and it will be opened to you" (Matthew 7:7). I ask that my grandchildren will pray to You, and seek You for everything, and knock on doors that only You can open. Close doors to them that cannot be opened because they lead to the production of bad fruit. Teach them to turn to You as the source of all good fruit in their lives.

In Jesus' name I pray.

If you abide in Me, and My words abide in you, you will ask what you desire, and it shall be done for you. By this My Father is glorified, that you bear much fruit; so you will be My disciples.

JOHN 15:7-8

Prayer Notes

_____

_____

_____

_____

_____

_____

_____

_____

_____

_____

_____

_____

Lord, Grow My Grandchildren's Faith to Believe That All Things Are Possible with You

Lord, I lift up my grandchildren to You today. (Name each grandchild before God.) Give them faith in You and Your Word that is strong enough to believe for miracles when they pray. Help them to always trust that nothing is impossible for You. Teach them that You are the God of the impossible. Help them to understand that their faith in You opens the door to a miraculous life. You have said in Your Word that "if you can believe, all things are possible to him who believes" (Mark 9:23). Enable my grandchildren to believe that there is nothing too hard for You, and all things are possible when they pray to You in faith.

In Jesus' name I pray.

Ah, Lord GOD! Behold, You have made the heavens and the earth by Your great power and outstretched arm. There is nothing too hard for You.

JEREMIAH 32:17

Prayer Notes

_____

_____

_____

_____

_____

_____

_____

_____

_____

_____

_____

Lord, Grow My Grandchildren's Faith to Believe That All Things Are Possible with You

Lord, enable my grandchildren to see how reading Your Word increases their faith. Jesus, You said, "If you have faith as a mustard seed," then "nothing will be impossible for you" (Matthew 17:20). Plant in each of my grandchildren a seed of faith that grows into giant faith that believes for miracles when they pray to You. Keep my grandchildren from ever losing hope in Your ability and desire to rescue them from any hopeless situation. I pray the same for their parents and for me. I ask that You, "the God of hope," will fill my grandchildren with joy and peace in believing so they can "abound in hope by the power of the Holy Spirit" (Romans 15:13).

In Jesus' name I pray.

Jesus looked at them and said, "With men it is impossible, but not with God; for with God all things are possible."

MARK 10:27

Prayer Notes

Other Books by Stormie Omartian

THE POWER OF A PRAYING® PARENT

Learn how to turn to the Lord and place every detail of your child's life in *His* hands by praying for such things as your child's safety, character development, peer pressure, friends, family relationships, and much more. Discover the joy of being part of God's work in your child's life. You don't have to be a perfect parent. You just need to be a praying parent.

THE POWER OF PRAYING® FOR YOUR ADULT CHILDREN

In this follow-up to *The Power of a Praying® Parent*, Stormie addresses areas of concern you may have for your grown children and shares how to effectively lift them up to God. It doesn't matter how young or old they are, you can rest in the power of God working through your prayers for them.

OUT OF DARKNESS

Stormie tells her compelling story with courage and transparency. Finding herself overwhelmed by depression, anxiety, and fear and on the verge of suicide, she shares the turning point that changed her life and reveals the healing process that brought freedom and wholeness beyond what she ever imagined. She tells of the restoration that happened as she was blessed with children and, later, grandchildren.